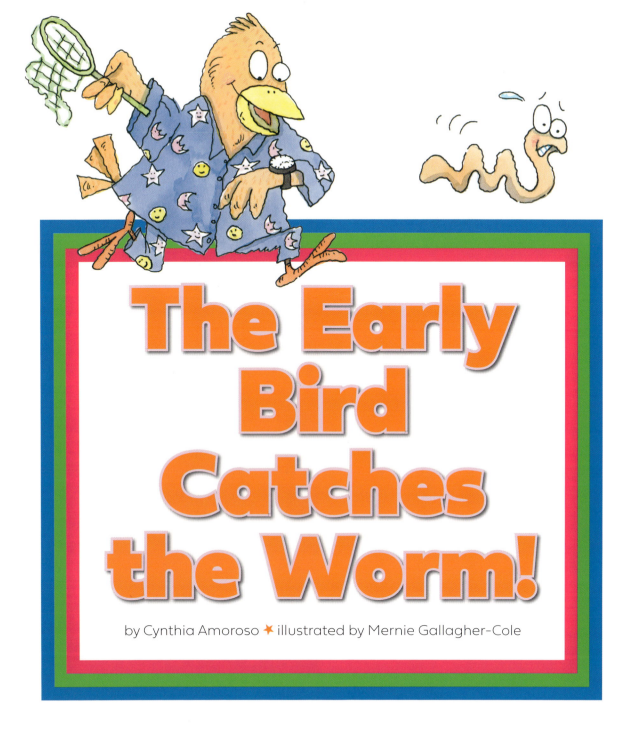

The Early Bird Catches the Worm!

by Cynthia Amoroso ★ illustrated by Mernie Gallagher-Cole

Wonder Books
An Imprint of The Child's World®
childsworld.com

Published by The Child's World®
800-599-READ • childsworld.com

Copyright © 2023 by The Child's World®
All rights reserved. No part of this book may be reproduced or utilized in any form of by any means without written permission from the publisher.

ISBN Information
9781503865655 (Reinforced Library Binding)
9781503866102 (Portable Document Format)
9781503866942 (Online Multi-user eBook)
9781503867789 (Electronic Publication)

LCCN 2022939698

Printed in the United States of America

ABOUT THE AUTHOR
As a daughter of elementary and English teachers, Cynthia Amoroso grew up in a home that was filled with language. She spent many hours enjoying reading and writing. Later, she followed in the footsteps of both her parents and became a teacher. As a high school English teacher and as an elementary teacher, Cynthia shared her love of language with students. She has always been fascinated with idioms and other figures of speech as they reflect and represent the culture and people who use them.

ABOUT THE ILLUSTRATOR
Mernie Gallagher-Cole lives in Pennsylvania with her husband and children. She uses idioms like the ones in this book every day. She has illustrated many children's books as well as greeting cards, puzzles, and games.

Contents

Ace in the hole 4
Blow off steam 4
Bolt from the blue 5
Brownie points 6
Cold shoulder 7
Cut-and-dried 7
Down the hatch 8
Dressed to the nines 9
The early bird catches the worm 10
Fly off the handle 11
A frog in my throat 11
Get your goat 12
Half the battle 13
Lead you by the nose 13
Let's get this show on the road 14
Mind your Ps and Qs 15
Monkey business 16
Off the deep end 17
Push the envelope 18
Roll with the punches 18
A shot in the dark 19
Smell like a rose 20
Tongue-in-cheek 21
When the cat's away 21

Glossary . . . 22
Wonder More . . . 23
Find Out More . . . 24
Index . . . 24

People use **idioms** every day. These are sayings and phrases with meanings that are different from the actual words. Some idioms seem silly. Many of them don't make much sense . . . at first.

This book will help you understand some of the most common idioms. The illustrations will show you how you might hear a saying or phrase. And the accompanying examples and definitions will tell you how the idiom is used, what it really means, and where it **originated**. All of these idioms—even the silly or humorous ones—are a rich, colorful part of the English language. You'll soon see that understanding idioms and knowing how to use them is a piece of cake!

Ace in the hole

The big baseball game was on Saturday. The Tigers were sure they would beat the Mustangs. But what the Tigers didn't know is that a home-run hitter had just returned to the Mustang team. He would be the Mustangs' ace in the hole.

MEANING: *To have something valuable that is kept secret until it is used; a hidden advantage*
ORIGIN: *This* **expression** *has been in use since the 1880s. It comes from the game of poker. The ace is the highest card in poker, and an "ace in the hole" can mean a winning hand.*

Blow off steam

Jake was mad. Everything had gone wrong today. He forgot his homework. He squirted ketchup on his shirt at lunch. He struck out in softball. He even missed the bus going home. Jake was getting angrier and angrier!

"What's the matter?" asked Dad at dinner. Jake couldn't stand one more thing. He told his dad everything that had gone wrong. By the time he was done talking, Jake was angry again.

"You need to blow off some steam," his dad replied. "Why don't you go outside and have fun. Ride your bike or take a jog. You'll feel much better."

MEANING: *To have an outburst of angry energy; to get rid of anger*
ORIGIN: *In the early days of locomotives, conductors would release steam to reduce built-up pressure in the engine.*

Bolt from the blue

George couldn't believe it. He had worked hard to be a good leader on his baseball team. He hoped to be voted captain this year. He was sure he would get it. The team voted. When the votes were counted, Jimmy had won. George was stunned. He told his uncle as soon as he got home.

"George, I'm sorry about what happened," his uncle said. "I know how much you wanted to be captain. You worked really hard for it. The vote for Jimmy must have been a bolt from the blue."

MEANING: *When something completely unexpected happens; sudden and shocking*
ORIGIN: *This expression has been in use since the early 1800s. Most people believe it started from the* literal *sense. In other words, a lightning strike on a clear day (a "bolt from the blue") would be surprising.*

Brownie points

Molly didn't like cleaning, but she'd been working on her room for hours. Now it was spotless. She was making her bed when she heard her mom come home.

"Hey Mom, I have a surprise for you!" she called out.

"Wow, this is great," said Mom when she saw the room. "You've really earned some brownie points today!"

MEANING: *To get credit for a good deed; doing something that makes someone else happy or that someone appreciates*

ORIGIN: *Brownies is a rank of the Girl Scouts. It is for young girls who aren't old enough to be Girl Scouts. The "points" refer to Brownies advancing levels or earning badges by doing various activities for their troop or community.*

Cold shoulder

"Can you believe Melissa is having a sleepover and didn't invite us?" asked Rachel.

"I know!" exclaimed Marsha. "We've been her best friends since we were three. Rachel is close friends with Benita now. Ever since Benita moved here, Rachel's been giving us the cold shoulder."

MEANING: *To ignore someone in a mean or hurtful way*
ORIGIN: *This phrase originated hundreds of years ago in Europe. It refers to kindness and* **generosity** *to strangers. When knights or other important people were traveling, they would often stop at castles or people's homes for a hot meal and rest. However, when common travelers passed through, they were served a cold dish of a shoulder of mutton (sheep). This less-welcoming meal was a way of letting the traveler know they needed to move on as soon as possible.*

Cut-and-dried

The citywide talent show was coming up, and Sara had ideas for some changes. "They'd make the show more interesting," she told her mom.

"Those are great ideas," said Mom, "but I don't think the committee will want to make changes this late. They've been doing this event the same way for years. Everything is pretty much cut-and-dried."

MEANING: *Prepared ahead of time and according to plan; not subject to change*
ORIGIN: *Many people believe the term originally referred to herbs for sale that were dried and cut. The first use of the expression was in a letter written in the early 1700s. A* **clergyman** *wrote that the sermon was "ready cut and dried," meaning that it was prepared ahead of time.*

Down the hatch

Ellen didn't like peas. It didn't matter if they were boiled or mashed. She didn't like them hot, and she didn't like them cold. She let them sit until they were the very last thing on her plate.

"Ellen, hurry up and eat your peas. We want to go to the movies," said Mom.

Ellen scooped up all of the peas in one spoonful. "Down the hatch!" she said as she swallowed them all.

MEANING: *To eat or swallow something, especially quickly or in one gulp*
ORIGIN: *This saying dates back to the mid-1500s. The "hatch" originally referred to an opening on the deck of a ship. Sailors and other crew members would put cargo and other items down the hatch of their ship.*

Dressed to the nines

It was Ramona's birthday. Her family was going to a nice restaurant and then to a play to celebrate. Ramona put on a beautiful new dress with new shoes that sparkled. She fixed her hair up with shiny ribbons.

Now Ramona just wished everyone else would hurry up! Finally she heard them coming downstairs.

"Wow!" exclaimed Dad when he saw Ramona. "You look terrific. You certainly are dressed to the nines tonight!"

MEANING: *To be very dressed up; to wear fancy clothes and look nice*
ORIGIN: *One **theory** about this idiom's origin is that it comes from the Old English saying "dressed to then eyne," which meant that a person was dressed beautifully from their toes to their eyes. Over time the word eyne shifted to nine.*

The early bird catches the worm

Gus wanted to go to the football game. The problem was that there weren't enough tickets for everyone. They were going on sale tomorrow at 10:00.

The next morning, Gus was dressed and ready to leave the house by 8:00.

"Where are you going?" asked his little brother, Billy.

"I'm going to get in line for football tickets," answered Gus.

"Why so early? You can't get them for two hours!" Billy said.

"That's right," agreed Gus. "But remember, the early bird gets the worm!"

MEANING: *If you do something early or ahead of time, you will succeed.*

ORIGIN: *Birds love to eat worms. If a bird shows up late in the day to a spot where worms are, the bird will go hungry. All the worms will have been eaten. Or the worms will have dug back under the ground. If the bird arrives early, it will likely get a meal of worms!*

Fly off the handle

Dad walked in the door from work. He looked tired.
    "Boy, am I glad to be home!" exclaimed Dad. "Things are so stressful at work. I just can't believe how people are acting. If one more person flies off the handle, I don't know what I'm going to do!"

MEANING: *To become upset or throw a tantrum; to act out of control, especially if you're angry*
ORIGIN: *In the early 1800s, many people used handmade tools. Often the tools were imperfect or faulty. As someone was chopping wood with an ax, the ax-head (the sharp blade) might loosen and come off— it would fly off the handle and be out of control.*

A frog in my throat

Elijah was supposed to give a book report in class. But he had a headache, and his throat felt scratchy.
    "My book—" he started, then stopped. His voice didn't sound right at all!
    "You sound as if you've got a frog in your throat," said Mrs. Hale. "Why don't you try a drink of water first?"

MEANING: *To have a hoarse voice or find it hard to speak*
ORIGIN: *This phrase became popular in the United States in the 1800s. The origin is unclear, but it most likely comes from the fact that someone with a hoarse voice might sound similar to a frog croaking.*

Get your goat

Ben was running out of patience. His little sister was bothering him on purpose. He couldn't take one more minute.

"Mom!" called Ben. "I'm trying to do my homework, and Ella won't leave me alone. She's doing everything she can think of to annoy me. Will you please make her stop?"

"Don't let her get your goat, Ben," said Mom. "Just ignore her. She'll get bored and go away."

MEANING: *To bother or annoy*

ORIGIN: *This is an American expression from the early 1900s. In horseracing it was a common practice to put a goat in the stall with the horse. The goat would help keep the horse calm before the race. But if someone wanted the horse to lose the race, they would sneak in the stall and take the goat away. This would really upset the racehorse!*

Half the battle

Diego and his family were on their way home from vacation. It had been a terrible morning! The rental car had a flat tire. Then Dad took a wrong turn on the highway. They barely made it to the airport in time.

"Whew," sighed Dad as they reached their plane's gate. "We made it! Just getting to the plane was half the battle. Now let's hope the flight goes smoothly, and we get all our luggage when we land!"

MEANING: *A successful start to something that takes time or energy; a successful beginning*

ORIGIN: *This phrase dates back to the 1700s. It refers to war and is a shortened version of the* **proverb**, *"The first blow is half the battle." In other words, if a soldier can make it through the first blows, or strikes, of fighting, that is often the hardest part.*

Lead you by the nose

Antonio was mad. David was always telling him what to do. Today it had gotten Antonio in trouble at school. Now he was trying to explain it to his dad.

"Antonio, you have to start standing up for yourself. You need to make your own decisions," his dad said. "Don't let David lead you by the nose."

MEANING: *Letting someone tell you what to do or not do; controlling someone*

ORIGIN: *Cattle and horses are sometimes led by a rope that's attached to a ring in their noses. This expression first appeared in the Bible. By the 1500s, its meaning referred to controlling other people.*

Let's get this show on the road

Ashley was excited. She and her family were going camping for a week! They'd been packing and getting ready for days. Now they were loading the last things into the camper.

"I think that's everything!" exclaimed Mom.

"It had better be! There's no room for anything else," answered Dad. "OK, everyone into the van. Let's get this show on the road!"

MEANING: *To get going or get moving; to start a task*

ORIGIN: *This popular expression refers to traveling shows. Before modern transportation like cars and airplanes, people didn't travel very often, especially not for entertainment. So the show, or entertainment, came to them. Carnivals, circuses, actors, and other performers would travel from town to town. When their show was over, the boss would say that it was time to get the show on the road. In other words, pack everything up and move on to the next place.*

Mind your Ps and Qs

Grace's dad was a teacher. Ms. Moss was the principal at his school. Grace had never met her. One day, she went to school with her father.

"Mind your Ps and Qs if we see Ms. Moss," said her father. "I've told her so many nice things about you!"

MEANING: *To do things right; to be very careful and pay attention; have good manners*
ORIGIN: *This popular expression has been used since the 1600s, but its exact origin is unclear. Some people believe that children learning the alphabet often mix up the letters p and q, so they need to look at, or mind, the letters carefully. Others say the phrase comes from English pubs. The bartender would write down the number of pints and quarts each customer drank on a blackboard to keep track of what they had to pay.*

Monkey business

Alex was bored. He was tired of working quietly at his desk. It was time to make some people laugh! He leaned over and told Nathan what he was going to do.
   "Alex, no monkey business! You're going to get in trouble!" warned Nathan.

MEANING: *To be silly; to get in trouble*

ORIGIN: *This expression has been popular in the United States since the 1900s. Its meaning is based on the fact that monkeys are known to be silly and playful. Many popular sayings compare animal behavior to human behavior, including "brave as a lion" or "slow as a snail."*

Off the deep end

The soccer game had not gone well. In fact, the whole season had not been a good one. Coach was fed up. After the game, he talked to the team. He got angrier and angrier. Soon he was yelling. His face got red, and he threw his hat on the ground. Finally he stormed off the field.

Sam turned to his teammate, Robbie. "I know we didn't play well today," he said, "but Coach sure is mad. I think he's gone off the deep end!"

MEANING: *To act in a way that seems out of control; to act without thinking of the end result*

ORIGIN: *The origin of this expression refers to a swimming pool's deep end. If you aren't a good swimmer, you should start off in the shallow area. You should not jump into the deep end first. You will be over your head and out of control.*

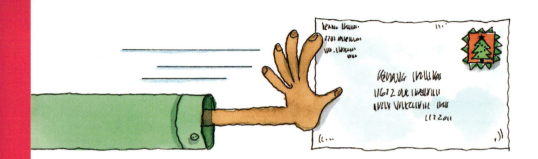

Push the envelope

Aiden was helping his uncle Matt hang Christmas lights. They were almost done, and there was only a short string of lights left to hang. Uncle Matt looked at it. Could he reach the end without moving the ladder? He stretched and stretched to clip the last two lights to the edge of the roof.

"Careful, Uncle Matt!" called Aiden. "Don't push the envelope! Let's move the ladder closer first."

MEANING: *To go to the limit; to go as far as it is safe*
ORIGIN: *This expression was created in the 1940s by people who worked in aviation. The term* flight envelope *referred to the air space (how high and low) where pilots could safely fly and* maneuver. *In training or testing aircrafts, pilots and engineers would test or "push" the limits of a flight envelope.*

Roll with the punches

Amanda and her parents sat in her classroom. It was her conference with the teacher. They had just moved to this new school a few weeks ago.

"I'm so proud of how well Amanda is doing," said Ms. Alvarez, Amanda's teacher. "It's not easy starting a new school in the middle of the year. But Amanda just rolls with the punches."

MEANING: *Not to let things bother you or get you down; to adjust to a difficult situation*
ORIGIN: *This saying comes from the sport of boxing. Boxers know that they have to move with the hits, or punches, from their opponent. They must duck, roll, or shift their body in a way to lessen the impact of the blow.*

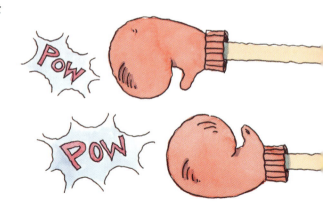

A shot in the dark

"That test was hard!" exclaimed Mara. "I studied all week, and I'm not sure how well I did."

"I thought it was OK," said Leo.

"Really? You told me you didn't study," Mara replied. "How did you even try answering the questions?"

"I just took a shot in the dark," answered Leo. "Hopefully I'll get lucky!"

MEANING: *A wild guess; to try to do something when you aren't sure if you can be successful*

ORIGIN: *If you are shooting at a target in the dark, you can't see where you are aiming. You are unlikely to succeed. The writer George Bernard Shaw is credited with using this phrase as a* **metaphor** *in his writings during the late 1800s.*

Smell like a rose

Evan was tired. He had dropped a bowl of salad all over the kitchen floor. Dressing splattered onto the cupboards. Lettuce and vegetables had scattered everywhere. Evan wiped down the cupboards and scrubbed the floor. Then he made a new salad. Finally everything was ready for dinner.

"Look at this kitchen," said Dad with a whistle. "Your mother is going to be surprised by how clean everything is! And the salad looks delicious."

"Will Mom be mad about the bowl I broke?" asked Evan.

"Oh, I don't think so," said Dad. He smiled. "In fact, I'd say you'll probably come out of this smelling like a rose."

MEANING: To end up in a good position; to look good in a bad situation

ORIGIN: This saying became popular in the United States during the early 1900s. Most people agree that the scent of a rose is pleasant. Today, if you come out of something smelling like a rose, it is **slang** for coming out of a situation better than expected.

Tongue-in-cheek

Zachary was growing fast, and he was hungry all the time.

"Would you like a sandwich?" his mom asked.

"I don't know," said Zachary. "Dad said that if I keep eating this much, he'll start taking grocery money out of my allowance!"

"Oh, he wasn't serious!" said Mom with a laugh. "He was just speaking tongue-in-cheek."

MEANING: Used to describe something said in a joking or teasing way; not serious

ORIGIN: This phrase was first used in the 1700s in England. It originally referred to the actual expression a person makes when they're saying something in an *ironic* way. What they say isn't serious or they are joking around.

When the cat's away . . .

Shauna was head of the decorations committee for the school dance. When she got home from their meeting, her dad asked how it went.

"It was tough!" Shauna said. "Everybody knew what they were supposed to do. But every time Mr. Roberts left the room, they all started messing around!"

"Oh, boy," said Dad. "I've seen that happen. When the cat's away . . . "

MEANING: When the person in charge is gone, people might not follow the rules; taking advantage of freedom

ORIGIN: The full saying of this proverb is, "When the cat's away, the mice will play." It has been in use since the 1600s and has appeared in many languages in different parts of the world. Its origin is rooted to relating animals to people. If a cat is in a house, a mouse will stay hidden. But if the cat is not around, the mouse will run free.

Glossary

clergyman (KLUR-jee-mun): An official member of a religious order; someone who has duties in a church.

expression (ek-SPREH-shun): A common saying; telling or showing your thoughts and feelings.

generosity (jen-ur-AH-sih-tee): Having a desire or willingness to give to or help others.

idioms (ID-ee-umz): Phrases or sayings whose meaning can't be understood by their individual words taken separately.

ironic (eye-RON-ik): Using words to express a meaning that is the opposite of their usual meaning, usually in a humorous way.

literal (LIT-er-uhl): Concerned with the facts and free from exaggeration; exact.

maneuver (muh-NOO-vur): Specialized movements or tactics; changing position for a purpose.

metaphor (MET-uh-for): Comparing two things by stating that one thing is the other thing.

originated (uh-RIJ-ih-nay-ted): To bring or come into being; to begin.

proverb (PRAH-vurb): A popular, often short saying that expresses something true and wise.

slang (SLANG): Informal speech; giving new meanings to old words or inventing new words.

theory (THEER-ee): A belief or an unproven assumption; a guess or estimate based on limited knowledge or information.

Wonder More

- Write a short story using an idiom. You can make up a story or use an experience from your own life. For example, if you choose the idiom "every cloud has a silver lining," you could write about discovering something good in an otherwise bad situation.

- In what ways do idioms impact our writing? In your opinion, do they help improve our ability to tell stories and describe events, or are they unnecessary? Explain your reasoning.

- Think of an idiom that isn't in this book and create a new entry. Write your own brief story using the idiom, and draw a picture to go with it. Then write down its meaning and origin. If you don't know the idiom's origin, where could you learn more about it?

- People often relate animal behavior to human behavior. And there are many animal-themed idioms. Pick out the animal idioms in this book. Which one do you relate to or like the most? Partner with someone in your class, and see how many animal idioms you can think of that are not in this book.

Find Out More

In the Library

Heinrichs, Ann. *Similes and Metaphors*. Mankato, MN: The Child's World, 2020.

Pearson, Yvonne, and Mernie Gallagher-Cole (illustrator). *Rev Up Your Writing in Fictional Stories*. Mankato, MN: The Child's World, 2016.

Schubert, Susan, and Raquel Bonita (illustrator). *I'll Believe You When . . . Unbelievable Idioms from around the World*. Minneapolis, MN: Lerner, 2020.

Zafarris, Jess. *Once Upon a Word: A Word-Origin Dictionary for Kids*. Emeryville, CA: Rockridge Press, 2020.

On the Web

Visit our website for links about idioms: **childsworld.com/links**

Note to Parents, Caregivers, Teachers, and Librarians: We routinely verify our Web links to make sure they are safe and active sites. So encourage your readers to check them out!

Index

ace in the hole, 4
ax-head, 11
Bible, the, 13
blow off steam, 4
bolt from the blue, 5
brownie points, 6
clergyman, 7
cold shoulder, 7
cut-and-dried, 7
down the hatch, 8
dressed to the nines, 9
early bird catches the worm, 10

fly off the handle, 11
frog in my throat, 11
generosity, 7
get your goat, 12
Girl Scouts, 6
half the battle, 13
horseracing, 12
ironic, 21
joking, 21
lead you by the nose, 13
let's get this show on the road, 14
lightning, 5

literal, 5
maneuver, 18
metaphor, 19
mind your Ps and Qs, 15
monkey business, 16
off the deep end, 17
pressure, 4
proverb, 13, 21
push the envelope, 18
roll with the punches, 18

Shaw, George Bernard, 19
shot in the dark, 19
silly, 16
slang, 20
smell like a rose, 20
success, 13, 19
tantrum, 11
theory, 9
tongue-in-cheek, 21
valuable, 4
when the cat's away, 21